The Way She Bloomed

Her way out of abuse became a journey of healing through conversations with God

Dianice Martir

ISBN: 978-1-960509-22-2

Writing Coach:
Drs. Luisette Kraal
Saved To Serve International Ministry (SSIM)

Contents

Section-5: *It's Time to Heal*

Section-6: *You Are Supported*

Section-7: *Pushing Through*

Section-8: Trust

Section-9: Take Your Power Back

Section-10: The return to love

Section-11: You Will Win In The End

Dedication

For every woman who stayed too long,
or feared she wouldn't survive the separation.
For the ones who lost themselves in the name of love.
For every soul in my family who experienced domestic violence
and didn't know their worth.
For my children—may the cycle end with me.
For my dear aunt, Shamile Scharbaai, a constant light in my
darkest moments, who held me without judgement and never
let me forget who I was.

Introduction

I never imagined my healing would begin with a pen. But in the quiet moments—when the pain felt too heavy, when I had no one to turn to—I began to write. And in the silence, something beautiful happened: I heard God. This book was born in those moments. Not out of strength, but out of a brokenness only God understood. Not because I had all the answers, but because I was searching for them. And slowly, word by word, the fog began to lift. Most of these pieces are not just my words—they are the answers I received from the divine while writing in my journal, pouring out my heart in the quiet.

It's like God was speaking directly to me, guiding me through the darkness with gentle whispers of hope and truth. This book is part of my healing journey too. Every word I wrote helped me breathe a little deeper, believe a little more, and begin to trust myself—and God—again. I'm still healing—but now, I'm healing out loud. If you are here, maybe you're searching too. Maybe you've stayed too long. Maybe you're tired. Maybe you've been made to feel small, unworthy, or invisible. This book is for you.

It's a reminder that even after pain, there is purpose. That your story doesn't end here. That your soul already knows the way forward—and you don't have to take the first step alone. Let these words be a hand to hold. You are not too far gone. You are not alone. And yes—you will bloom too.

Section-1

The Ending That Freed Her

" *Where the breaking point*

transforms into a breakthrough. "

Waiting Was the Enemy

After years,
waiting for him to change.
Waiting for him to be as good as his words.
Waiting for the day he'd finally control his anger,
instead of taking it out on you.
Waiting for things to become what you hoped for—
all of it
just an illusion.

Eventually,
you realize...
waiting was never worth it.
Waiting was the enemy.
Because the enemy
was the one you were waiting for.

You were never meant to wait for love to feel safe.
You're not wrong for hoping.
You're not wrong for staying.
You're human.

And now you are free to choose you!

Speak this into your life:
I let go of the illusion and embrace reality with love for myself.

Why?

Babe, don't ask why.
Let him go.

You didn't feel safe in that relationship anyway;
you could never trust him;
everything was a lie anyway.
You weren't happy anyway;
you didn't like the way he treated you anyway.
All alone,
wondering what you did to deserve all that,
questioning your worth to a liar and abuser
who doesn't even know how to love himself,
let alone love others.
So stop wondering why.
God is pulling you out of what was never
meant to hold you.
And walking away?
That was the beginning of choosing your freedom.

Speak this into your life:
I recognize my value and deserve more.

His Choice

Babygirl,
I know maybe you wanted him by your side all along.
But,
as painful as this may sound,
it wasn't meant to be.
After all,
it was his choice to treat you like dirt.
It was his choice not to value you.
It was his choice not to love you.
So it's definitely his choice
that he can't come with you
to where I'm taking you next.

Speak this into your life:

My journey continues without those who choose not

to appreciate my worth.

He chose to let me go; I choose to rediscover myself.

The Difference

You were on the level with him.
You gave your all to be good enough for him.
You even permitted him to cross your boundaries.

And still,
he tried to break you.

You stayed.
You tried.
Again and again,
you gave your all.
You stayed loyal.
You were love.
He crossed the line.
But now,
God is going to build you back even stronger.

Because here's the difference:
Now,
you're done trying to be good enough for someone
who was never good enough for you.
Now,
you're good enough for yourself.

Speak this into your life:
What broke me has built me. I rise stronger and wiser.

This Was her Last Time

She told herself
that this time
he could come back
but only on her terms.
She promised herself
that this time,
she would be bold.
She would speak her truth.
She believed he would listen this time.
This time,
she would fight back.
And after this time,
there would be no more problems.
But if only she had known—
this time
would be her last.
Because this time,
she wouldn't get the chance
to leave again.

Speak this into your life:

I deserve a love that is free from pain. I refuse to return to suffering while pretending it is love.

Grief Is Necessary

It's okay to grieve.
Grieve the time you lost.
Grieve the trust you gave so freely.
Grieve the disappointment—that things didn't
turn out the way you hoped.
Grieve the love you showed to the wrong person.
The money you spent on the wrong person.
All the years spent in fear.
Grieve what could've been, if you had never met this
person.
Grieve the version of you that existed before you met
him.
Grieve that you couldn't change him.
That the future you imagined is no longer possible.
Grieve the loss of connection with family and friends.
The social isolation.
The loss of control over your own life.
And the guilt and shame of staying too long.

Grieve.
Cry it out.
And don't look back in blame.
You did what you had to do to survive.
The new you is waiting.

Speak this into your life:

I honor every aspect of my journey, including the pain that has

shaped who I am today.

Section-2

Gaslighting

"*Healing begins when truth finds its voice.*"

There's Nothing Wrong with You

You saw what you saw
But he said,
"It wasn't there."

You heard what you heard
But
"You were wrong."
You felt what you felt
And still,
according to him,
"You're being dramatic."
You're "crazy."
You're "overthinking too much."

Suddenly,
he was the victim.

And just like that,
everything was off the table.
Everything was denied.
Nothing happened.
Leaving you helpless,
and questioning your own mental health.

I'm here to tell you:
Girl, there's nothing wrong with you.
Let me introduce you
to Mr. Gaslight.

Speak this into your life:

I peel away every lie and find nothing but beauty underneath.

Being Silent Was Safe

You questioned every word you spoke.
Wondered if your feelings were too much—
too loud,
too sensitive—
until silence
became safer.

He told you:
"You're remembering it wrong."
"You're too emotional."
"You're making things up."
"You're being delusional."

And you began to wonder—
Am I?

Your truth.
Your gut.
Your reality—
all twisted and manipulated.

But deep down,
you knew
the story you told yourself...
was real.

Speak this into your life:
I speak my truth with courage and clarity.

Crazy? No. Just Caring

You were never crazy.
Never too much.
You were just too trusting.
Too kind.
Too forgiving—
for someone who didn't value your heart.

Speak this into your life:

I choose to love myself with the same depth that I once

gave to the wrong person.

Whispers of Doubt

Doubting yourself was never
a seed you planted in your heart.

But he whispered—
and you listened—
until it grew,
like vines around your confidence.

Doubting yourself
was never the weight you were meant to carry.
But the lies became your shadow,
and you began to shrink in their presence—
uncertain of your own reflection.

Doubting yourself
was never your fate to accept.
It was theirs to own.

Now, it's time to rise,
to remember who you are,
and reclaim the truth they tried to steal.

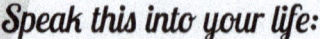

Speak this into your life:
*I trust the voice within. Even in silence, I hear my
worth loud and clear.*

Just Asking

He said that he loved you.
So why does it feel like he wants to break you?

He said he wants to be with you—and only you.
So why does he keep telling you you're "too difficult"?

He said:
"You can talk to me about everything,"
but somehow,
you end up feeling crazy and stupid instead.

He said he wants to make things right—
but only if you neglect your boundaries.

He said he wants to marry you,
but he's the only one allowed to be in control.

And you said,
"I just want to be happy."

But how far are you willing to let him go?
How much more will you shrink yourself?
Are you sure you don't deserve better?

Just asking...

Speak this into your life:

From now on, I will trust the questions in my heart –
they are the doorway to clarity.

It's Not You

Reject the idea that you should question your worth.

That self-doubt was imposed on you—
it's not who you really are.

You are enough.
You always were—
even when he made you doubt it.

Your voice.
Your strength.
Your worth.

Can NEVER be gaslit again.

Speak this into your life:
I embrace relationships that are founded on mutual
respect and emotional safety.

Gifts Don't Heal

You don't need more chocolate.
No need for more flowers.
No need for empty words.
They can't mask the hurt he caused.
Let him keep the fancy jewelry.
His words and actions left scars untold.
Make-up sex won't erase what he's done.
You don't need another apology
or empty promises
wrapped in a bow.
They won't heal the bruises
on your mind,
your body,
your soul.
Honestly,
he keeps buying your silence,
hoping you'll stay,
hoping you'll forget.
But all the gifts can't take the pain away.

The real gift?
You. Healing. Rising.
Becoming her again.

Speak this into your life:
I gift myself the love, peace and clarity I deserve.

Strength to Heal

I believe you.
It's not your fault.
Your perception is real.
You aren't crazy.

Your voice matters.
Your thoughts matter.
Your truth matters.
Your feelings are valid.

You are not delusional.
You are bigger than his manipulations.

It's okay to set boundaries.
You are worthy of love and respect.
It's okay to trust your instinct.
You don't have to justify your feelings to anyone.

You have the strength to rediscover yourself.
You have the strength to heal.

Speak this into your life:
I honor my past with compassion and step into my future with
power.

You Deserve Better

"The moment you choose yourself is the moment your life begins to shift. You deserve better, and your soul knows it."

Undesired Energy

Forget that mess.

You don't need his negative energy around you.
And definitely not inside of you.

The moment you release what drains you,
you make room for what restores you.

Protect your space.
Protect your body.
Protect your peace.

You deserve better.
Always have!

Speak this into your life:

Every choice I make now reflects the depth of my self-worth.

One Last Chance

For what?
To make you believe that this time everything will change?
That things will finally be different?
One more chance to deceive you?
To lie?
To cheat on you?
To beat you down one last time?
For you to be shattered in pieces again?
To ignore your feelings, your emotions, your truth?
One more chance to prove—again—that he doesn't care?
One more shot at controlling you, disrespecting you, making you question yourself?

NOT THIS TIME!

You don't owe him another damn chance to hurt you again.
The only chance being given now is the one you're giving yourself.

To heal.
To breathe again.
To rise in your worth.

Because **you deserve a chance too!**

Speak this into your life:
This time, the chance is mine-and I'm not wasting it on pain.

Never Again

Nobody has the right to treat me like I'm worthless.
Nobody has the right to make me feel small,
to make me feel afraid.

And once I fully discover who I am—
who I've always been beneath the pain—

I will never, ever
allow anyone to mess with me like that again.

Never again!

Speak this into your life:

I recognize my worth, and I refuse to shrink myself for anyone.

Ever again.

The Blessing of Walking Away

And you, my queen:
Straighten your crown.
Lift your chin.
Pull those shoulders back.
Let your smile shine.
Walk away with grace,
with power,
with faith,
and with trust—

Like you're on a catwalk of purpose
in the right direction this time.
With each step saying:
I'm choosing me now.
Because this pain will pass,
but your power—your light—that stays.

He didn't give you your light,
so he doesn't get to take it.

Let it shine again.
Walk in it.
Think in it.
Live in it.

Be patient with yourself.
What God is preparing for you
is more beautiful than anything you had to let go.

You haven't lost.
You've been redirected.
Believe that you deserve so much better
than what broke you.

You are too valuable—too divine—
to stay anywhere that doesn't honor who you truly are.

Speak this into your life:

I left the pain but I took my crown with me.

This walk is not just away from him, it's toward everything I deserve.

Girl Look, Listen, READ!

If you've made the choice:

To make yourself the number one priority in your life.
To genuinely start loving yourself more than anything
and anyone.
To care about your mental and physical health.
To accept yourself as you are.
To wake up to your true power, your true value, your true
potential.
To heal yourself.

Then hear me clearly:

You are vibrating on a higher frequency now.
And the Universe responds to frequency.
That means the people in your life who are still
vibrating low—
those who betrayed you,
abused you,
humiliated you, belittled you, and tried to dim your light—
they will fall off.
They'll be removed.

Why?
Because they no longer match the energy you are
sending out.

They will be replaced
by people who will love you the way you want, need, and
deserve to be loved.
People who respect you and your boundaries.

People who lift you up and truly care for you.
The Universe will bring you people, experiences,
and blessings that match your new energy.

But you have to allow it to happen.

PLEASE UNDERSTAND THIS:
You are valuable.
You are worthy.
You are precious.
You matter.
A lot!

Now take a deep breath, and let that sh–t go!
Inhale through your nose and exhale through your
mouth.
On the exhale, say in your mind: I let that sh–t go.
Repeat as many times as you desire.

Go have a beautiful day, sweety!
SMILE.
You deserve it!

Speak this into your life:
I am valuable. I deserve so much better!

That Someone...

You deserve someone who:

Sees you.
Hears you.
Cares for you.
And truly values you.

Someone who treats you with love,
kindness,
and the deepest respect!

Speak this into your life:

I am worthy of love that sees, hears and honors me.

Section-4

Letting Go

"You've cried.

You've fought.

You've tried.

Now, it's time to let go.

Breathe, let go and rise."

Forced to Lose Hope

You devoted yourself
to breaking the cycle in your family—
no more kids being raised
in a one-parent household.

You wanted your children to grow up with a father
who was emotionally and physically present.

You thought he'd be your last, your forever—
maybe even your husband,
the one whose ring you'd wear.

The little crumbs of love and attention—
just enough to make you feel good every now and then.

But eventually,
you had no choice
but to let those hopes go.

Because instead of building you,
he began to crash your soul.

Speak this into your life:

I let go of the hopes that kept me trapped and embraced peace

that sets me free.

It's a Blessing to Cry

Cry it all out—
the memories,
the love he promised,
the chances you gave,
the life you never had together,
what no longer belongs to you.

Cry it out, girl—
all the pain and sadness you wore,
all the frustrations you kept inside for too long,
the false hopes you carried.

Let it all out.
Crying is necessary for your healing.
Have a good cry.
Allow that energy to leave your body through your tears.

And when you're done...

Remind yourself:

Love doesn't hurt like that.
it's a blessing to cry.

Speak this into your life:

With every tear, I return closer to myself.

I rise stronger after every storm.

Let Go and Let God

I cannot let you stay in that situation, my love.
I cannot allow anyone to mishandle you like that.
You are important.
You matter.
You are far too valuable.
Far too precious to Me.
I understand you, sweety.
And you will later understand
why you stayed for so long,
and why it's time for you to leave now, baby.
You are going to be fine.
I will carry you through this—
but you, my love,
must also choose to cooperate
with your own healing and well-being.
It's not easy, I know.
But if you only trust Me—
trust Me wholeheartedly and be patient,
you will start to see miracles unfold in your life.

Believe Me when I say:
you will rise from this—
stronger, wiser, and brighter than ever.

Speak this into your life:

This ending is not my failure; it's my beginning!

Detachment Is Healing

When you are healing,
it's important—and necessary—
to have boundaries with people
who continuously and intentionally hurt you.
You have to remove yourself from the toxic environment
if you truly want to start feeling better !

Speak this into your life:

When love turns into control, I walk away. When peace is missing,

I draw the line.

I set holy boundaries and walk away from what dims my light.

Leave It All Behind

Eliminate all thoughts,
all things,
and all people that drain your energy.
Let go of everything that's not in alignment
with who you are or who you want to become.
These things are robbing you of your joy,
they are robbing you of your peace,
and of your self-love.
They stand in the way of your true purpose
and keep you from living your full potential.
It's time to stand in your power!

Speak this into your life:

I let go of what no longer serves me and make space for peace,

joy and purpose.

Don't Be Surprised

When you truly begin to love yourself—
When you start embracing your inner beauty,
When you set firm boundaries for how you want to be treated,
When you deepen your awareness
and accept that you are beautiful and worthy,
When you start thinking highly of yourself
and believing the TRUTH about who you really are...

You'll realize you DESERVE good things,
real experiences, and
genuine people in your life.

But here's the thing—
You HAVE to be prepared to let go of some of the people closest to you.

Unfortunately,
those are often the ones you loved the most.
The ones you stayed loyal to.
The ones you hoped would change.
The ones you believed you had a deep connection with.

But they are also the ones who mistreated you,
used you,
lied to you,
manipulated you.
They did everything to break you down mentally and
emotionally.
They never really cared for you—
unless it served them.

They took advantage of your
lack of confidence,
your lack of self-love.
Most of the time, you felt very anxious and insecure
around them.

To them, you were never a priority.
You were just an option.

Speak this into your life:

As I rise in love with myself, only those who rise with me can stay.

So Much More

Let go, sweety.

You are so much more than this pain.

So much more
than all the thoughts and scenarios you keep replaying
in your mind.

You are not losing.
You're making space for what you truly deserve.

Let it go.
Trust—
and let the Universe do its work.

The Universe never takes without giving more in return.

Speak this into your life:
I trust that something better is already on its way to me.

When He Chose Her

Sometimes we think we're being replaced,
when in fact—we're being rescued.

Especially when you've been praying or meditating,
asking God to free you from the hands of your abuser.

The truth is:
Sometimes God will purposefully
place another woman in a man's life,
just to save your life.

She got him. You got free.

God let him go.

Speak this into your life:

His choice was my liberation. God stepped in when I was

unable to walk away.

Shift Your Focus

Don't focus on him anymore.
Don't sit around waiting for him to be punished either.
And definitely don't try to punish him yourself.

It's not worth your time or energy.
Stop wasting your precious energy on people and things
that aren't aligned with your well-being.
He doesn't deserve that much space in your mind.

Keep moving forward with a pure heart.
God has it from here.

Speak this into your life:
I trust in the divine timing of my healing and let go of
all that weighs me down.

Section-5

It's Time to Heal

"*You are not just healing -*
You're returning to the
woman God created you to be"

Because YOU Deserve Peace

FORGIVE him without judgment.
You don't have to understand his choices.
You only have to choose yourself.
You're freeing yourself from the pain—
because you deserve to breathe again.
And to heal.

Speak this into your life:

Forgiveness liberates me, not them.

I Am Enough

You are ENOUGH.
You are LOVED.
You are APPRECIATED.

Speak this into your life:

I embrace the truth of who I am – Whole, worthy and complete.

You Are Overqualified

Stop searching for reasons and excuses why you're not
good enough.
You are more than good enough—for me,
and for those who truly see you.

Love yourself.
Cherish yourself, baby.
Don't be so hard on that beautiful heart.

Remember who you are:
A daughter of the Creator.
A Princess.

Be patient with yourself.
You are more than enough.
Don't forget it!

Speak this into your life:

I am deserving of what is meant for me.

Nothing Changed

The heartbreak didn't lower your value.
It didn't dim your light.
You are still worthy.
You are still beautiful.
You are still magnificent.
You still have that glow.
STILL THAT QUEEN.

Speak this into your life:

Heartbreak cannot lessen my worth.

The Chains Are Broken

Now is the time
to start working on yourself—
not because you're broken,
but because you are finally free.
Free to grow into everything they said you couldn't be.
Use this freedom wisely,
because it's yours for a reason.

Speak this into your life:

Each step I take towards my healing, is proof that

I'm no longer stuck.

It's Me Time Now

This is your time.

Your time to grow.
Your time to heal.
This is the time for your soul to evolve—
the time for you to learn how to value yourself.

You've already been through so much.
Please, be gentle with yourself.
Love yourself.
Be kind to yourself.

You're not just surviving,
you are becoming the woman you once prayed to be.

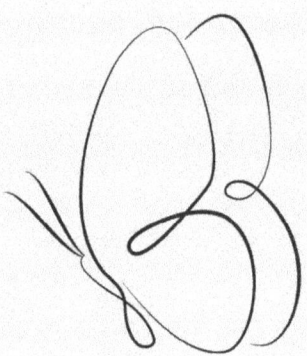

Speak this into your life:

*I honor this season of growth and give myself all the love
I once gave away.*

Healing Changes Everything

Heal, sweety,
so you can overcome the fears
that were born from your brokenness—
the fear of not being good enough,
the fear of being abandoned,
the fear of being hurt again.

Heal so those fears no longer lead your life.
So you can finally breathe, trust,
and enjoy all the wonders
that love, peace, and freedom bring.

Because healing doesn't mean you'll never feel fear—
it means fear won't control you anymore.

Speak this into your life:

I choose healing, not fear!

The Bloom Within

Look at you—
healing and growing,
even when no one is watching.

Choosing to break old patterns,
to free your mind,
to elevate yourself,
to rise above the noise.

You are blossoming—
not because life has been easy,
but because you refused to stay buried.

This journey isn't always loud,
but every step, every breath,
is proof of your becoming.

Be proud of your bloom, my love.
It's happening from the inside out.

Speak this into your life:
I bloom with purpose, grace and power.

Section-6

You Are Supported

" As you heal, remember:

You are never alone.

Support is all around you "

Let God Fight for You

Remember who you are.
Remember whose daughter you are.

You are not alone.

I need you to stay calm.
BREATHE.

Give your battle to God
Hand over all your sadness—
your thoughts, your emotions, your pain.

He will figure it out.
Let God fight for you.

And I promise—this will turn out in your favor.
Everything will be okay.

Trust and believe.

Speak this into your life:

I give my pain, worries and emotions to God,
knowing He will transform them.

God Don't Play About His Daughters

Dear beautiful woman,
You belong to the MOST HIGH.

How incredible is that?
How amazing is that?
How powerful is that?

You are the daughter of the King of all kings,
Queen of all queens.
You carry royalty in your DNA, baby.

You are His little princess.
That's why you're lifted and carried by His love.
That's why you're supported.
That's why you're surrounded by people who love you
unconditionally.
Their love is pure.

You are beautiful.
You have the strength to rise.
You are strong.
You are full of joy, happiness, and love to share with your
loved ones.

Breathe, baby!
And keep moving forward.

Speak this into your life:

I walk with the confidence of a daughter of the Most High.

Let Him Lose You

Anyone who wants to leave your life—

Let them!

Especially when your intentions were pure,
and they kept disappointing you.

Let him go.

Because I will hold your hand
and walk beside you.
I will carry you through every hardship.
You are not alone.
I will stand by your side
in every situation.

Let him leave—

So YOU can finally be free!

Speak this into your life:
I walk forward in faith, hand in hand with the One who guides me.

Backed Up by Source

God is manifesting Himself through you.
You belong to Him.
And don't you think He will take care of His own?
You are fully covered.
Protected.
Held.
He will never leave you helpless.

Speak this into your life:

I show up for life boldly, trusting that God always back me up.

Embrace Your Strength...

YOU ARE FREE.
YOU ARE SAFE.
YOU ARE PROTECTED.
YOU ARE STRONG.
YOU ARE LOVED.

Speak this into your life:

I embrace the strength that resides within me and surrounds me.

And to the Mothers

I love you.
I respect you.
I am so proud of you.
I know you're feeling sad right now.
Things are not how you wanted them to be.
But don't lose your faith.
You're doing the best you can, sweetheart,
and that's all you can do right now.
And it's okay!
I appreciate you.
Thank you for taking care of those kids.
Thank you for being here for them.
You are doing a great job, my love.
Just breathe!
Come back to yourself.
And remember who you are.
You are divine light.
You are a queen of love.
You've got this, sweetheart.
Again, I appreciate you.

Thank you for making their life possible here on Earth.
Thank you for allowing them to come here through you.
It's not easy.
I know and I understand.
But know that I've equipped you with all the strength and
wisdom you need to do this on your own.
I've got your back.
You can do it!

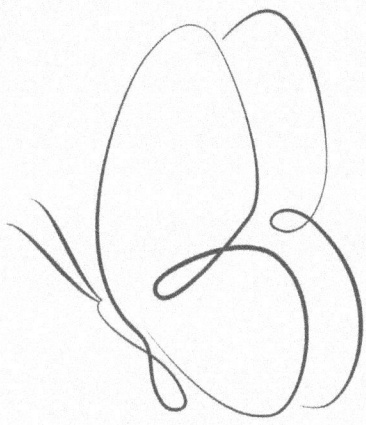

Speak this into your life:

Even on the hardest days, I am not alone. Heaven helps me raise

these children in love.

You Are Well Protected

You are an expression of God.
No one can tear you down.

If they come for you,
they'll have to answer to the One—
greater and stronger than anyone else:
The Almighty.

Speak this into your life:

No one can knock me down, for I am supported by the Almighty.

Section-7

Pushing Through

"*What broke you prepared you.*
What hurt you awakened you.
Now–walk in your God-given power."

Focus On the Good

Focus on what fills your heart with joy.
Focus on what makes you feel loved,
what brings light to your life.

When you shift your focus to the good,
you'll begin to attract more of it.

And no matter what you're facing,
you'll be able to fully embrace and enjoy those
moments.

Remember,
you are strong,
and you can handle whatever comes your way!

Speak this into your life:

*Every day, I find new reasons to smile and appreciate the
beauty around me.*

Eyes On The Bright Side

Leave the past where it belongs — behind you.
Free yourself, baby girl.

Keep your eyes on the light at the end of the tunnel.

Speak this into your life:
I am resilient, and my future is filled with hope and opportunity.

Shifting Forward

Don't linger in your pain.
You've carried it long enough.
The lessons have been learned.
Now, it's time to move on and grow.

Speak this into your life:

I am evolving. I step into the unknown with courage and faith.

The Strongest Soldier

You were built for this life
and for every lesson that comes with it.

You will never face anything you cannot handle.

This hardship you've endured
was meant to make you:
More resilient.
More self-assured.
More aware
that you are not to be played with.

Speak this into your life:

Every battle I've faced is shaping me into the warrior

I was born to be.

Pain Also Means Growth

Don't be upset,
This pain is not here to break you.
It's here to build you.
It's not punishment,
It's preparation.
God is testing you, stretching you,
shaping you,
Calling you higher.
Every challenge is leveling you up.
Don't fold now!
You're almost there.
Trust Him!

Speak this into your life:

*I embrace growth, even when it arises from challenges. I trust that
the process is preparing me for greater opportunities.*

Keep Pushing

I know it's hard, and really painful.
But you can't stop pushing now.
Just like a woman in labor:
The closer she gets to the birth, the more painful it
becomes.
But she can't stop.
She must TRUST her midwife to help deliver the baby
safely.
And when the baby is finally born,
the pain she had to endure
is nothing compared to the **immense joy**
of holding her newborn in her arms.
So please,
Hang in there, sweetie.
You have to push through, my love.
You are birthing something beautiful and real—
the you who's been hidden beneath the hurt, now rising
in power.
Don't give up now.
Put all your TRUST in God and
BELIEVE that you have all the strength you need for this
process.

You will bloom through the breaking,
Rise through the pain.
You will prosper.
You will win in the end.
Victory is already written—
And it has your name on it.

Speak this into your life:

I push through with grace and strength, knowing that something beautiful is being born from within me.

Be Open to Receive

Go on with your life,
And open your heart to the blessings coming your way.
Let go of any doubts
or fears that might hold you back
from receiving what's meant for you.
You gave your all,
now, it's your time to receive.
Accept all the blessings fully.
Embrace the abundance around you,
because you truly deserve it.
Know that God is always supporting you,
and everything you need is already on its way to you.

Speak this into your life:

I am deserving of all the good that comes my way.

Section-8

Trust

"There's a deeper knowing within you.

Trust it. The path is already blessed."

God Will Handle It

It's okay, my love.
It's okay, sweety.
Don't worry about anything.
It's not fair—
But let it be.
Move forward with your life, sweety.
Trust God.
Everything will be okay.
Don't stress.
Don't hold on to hate.
Just let it go and let it be.
God will handle it.
You are important.
You are needed.
That's why God is caring for you so deeply.

Speak this into your life:

I let go of what's not mine to carry and trust that justice flows in divine timing.

Fall To Rise

You are not any less.
You are beautiful.
You are growing—
connecting more and more with your higher self.
Don't let anyone take that away from you.
Don't allow anyone to stand in the way of your growth.
I know it hurts,
but it won't hurt forever.
You will overcome this.
Breathe!
Let go of that feeling.
Get up!
Keep going!
Move forward with trust in your heart,
believing that better is on the way.
Look for the lesson in this experience.
Learn, prepare yourself.
Because better is on the way.
Don't worry—
I got you!
And when I tell you not to worry,
it's because I know exactly what I'm doing.
Just trust me.

Speak this into your life:

The lessons I learn today are shaping the person I am becoming.

Let It Unfold

Trust the process.
Go with the flow.

Speak this into your life:

I trust the journey of my life.

Embrace Your Journey

Be proud of who you are and the woman you are
becoming.
Love yourself unconditionally, through
every step of your journey.
The process isn't always easy,
but it's all shaping you into the person you are
destined to be.
Trust that everything happening in your life is part of
your growth.
Trust that you are exactly where you need to be.
Each day brings you closer to the version of yourself
you've always dreamed of becoming.
So, take a deep breath and allow yourself to
grow at your own pace.
You are doing the work.
And in time,
you will see the beautiful changes unfolding within you.

Speak this into your life:

I honor my journey and celebrate how far I've come.

Leap of Faith

You are not meant to overthink everything.
You are meant to TRUST—
To trust the timing,
To trust the process,
To trust that God has something better for you.
Even when you can't see it yet,
Even when it feels uncertain.
Believe anyway.
Take the leap—
Faith will carry you.

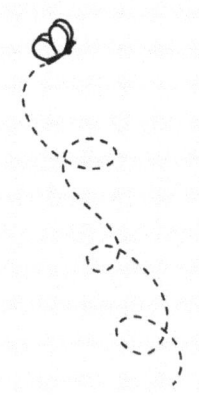

Speak this into your life:

I walk by faith, not by sight. My future is safe in God's hands.

Trust and Believe

You are loved.
You are supported.

Focus your mind on what truly matters.

Focus on what you want to attract into your life:
Peace, love, joy, harmony, abundance, good health.
I know it's hard to believe and trust right now,
because the future feels uncertain.

But I can tell you this:
It's beautiful.
It's going to be amazing.

The pain and sadness you're carrying aren't worth it.
Make peace with where you are.

Accept it.
Let go.

And create space for better things to come your way.

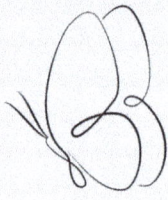

Speak this into your life:
I focus on the beauty around me, embracing life with
gratitude and wonder.

Section-9

Take Your Power Back

"With every tear you shed,
you watered the ground
you now rise from.
This is your becoming!"

Be Assured of Your Own Self-Worth

You are worth more than diamonds and gold.
There's absolutely nothing—
and no one—
that can take your value and worthiness away from you.

Speak this into your life:

My worth is untouchable- No one's actions, silence or

betrayal can ever take it from me.

Alchemize Your Pain

I know it hurts,
But love-
Let this be what lifts you.
Let this be the reason
you go harder
you dream bigger
you demand more.
Turn the pain into power.
Turn this heartbreak into hunger.

Use every scar as a steppingstone.
There is wisdom in the wounds.
There is beauty in beginning again.
Use this lesson as a catalyst for change.
Let it upgrade you.

Let it guide you into deeper healing of your heart,
your inner child,
your entire self.
Invest in your growth.
Rebuild your values.
Tend to your physical and mental health.
Baby, you're an alchemist.
You hold the power to turn pain into purpose.
And you will.

Speak this into your life:

I transform my pain into power and my wounds into wisdom.

Stronger Than They Ever Knew

Never underestimate yourself again.
You've been through the storm
and yet here you are, standing.
You cried, you broke,
You've carried pain in silence and still showed up,
You healed, you rose.
That wasn't the storm breaking you—
It was clearing the path for your light.
Now you see what you're made of.
Now you feel your own strength.
This is the version of you
That no longer doubts her power.
You were powerful all along—
you just needed the storm to remember.

Speak this into your life:

I trust in my ability to overcome and thrive.

This Pain Is Your Motivation

Alchemize it.
Let that hurt be fuel for your elevation.
Use every brick and stone they throw at you
to build one more step toward greatness.
Create a bridge of strength with them.
A tremendous blessing and immense joy
await you on the other side of this pain.
Let him think he's shining right now.
Let him think he's left you broken,
while you use this heartbreak to grow
wiser and more resilient.
Your time to shine will come.
And when it does, you will shine brighter than ever.

Speak this into your life:

I rise from the ashes of my pain, prepared to shine brighter than

ever before.

Fear Is an Illusion

Fear is just a thought.
You don't have to accept it.
Don't let fear control you.
Stop allowing yourself to suffer, sweetheart.
It's all in your mind.
Take control over your thoughts.
Take control over your fears.
You are the captain of your mind.
Don't let negativity take over.
God is with you.
God protects you.
God will heal you.

Speak this into your life:

Fear does not define me; my inner power does.

Go Within

Your higher self is so much more
than all those negative thoughts and emotions.
Listen to your inner voice.
Listen to your intuition.
Because that's where your power lives.
She whispers the truth you've always carried.
She is you,
Unshaken,
Undefeated and
Unbreakable.

Speak this into your life:

Every answer I seek is already inside me.

This Is Not the End

It's okay, babygirl.
BREATHE
Be patient with yourself.
Mind your thoughts.
Fight all the negative feelings and emotions away—
send them off,
return them back to their sender.
Babygirl, you're about to be elevated.
You're about to be upgraded.
It's time, sweety.
It's time for you to start celebrating again.
You are strong.
You are powerful.
You are magnificent.
You are magical.
You possess the power to change anything you wish:
your thoughts, your feelings, your habits, your focus, your
situation.
Anything, my dear.
You got this!
Welcome in your new life.
Welcome in your new season.
Don't worry about the other side.
You are free to grow now.
This is not the end of your story.
Your story shall continue.
Your story shall continue to be beautiful.

Speak this into your life:

God's light leads me to success and peace,
no matter the challenge.

Choose Yourself

When you choose yourself,
You honor your Creator.
Choose yourself over everything and everyone.
Choose yourself over and over again.

The people who hurt you
choose to do what they do—
and they may not even care about your feelings.

So in return,
how difficult it may seem,
YOU HAVE TO CHOOSE YOURSELF.

That isn't selfish—
that's self-love.

Choose you this time.

Speak this into your life:
I choose myself today and everyday moving forward.

Section-10

The return to love

"You've battled enough,
beautiful soul.
Now return to the truth-
You were always love."

She Was Always Love

You are love.
Love is your essence.
You were made of love, from love, with love.
Your truest self is love.
Everything about you, my dear—
is love.

You hold within you the power to be free.
To love yourself again.
To return to who you truly are:
Love.

It's already in you.
Just turn inward.
Focus on your heart—
and you will feel it.
You will know.

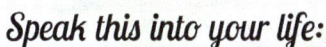

Love yourself
day by day—
each day,
a little more.

Speak this into your life:

Each breath of love brings me closer to the unstoppable

woman I am destined to become.

Start Loving You

Start loving you.
How people treat you has nothing to do with your worth.
Their actions reflect them—not your value.
So don't take it personally.
Don't carry what was never yours to hold.

You are still worthy.
Still radiant.
Still deserving of love that sees you,
respects you,
and holds you with care.

Start seeing yourself through loving eyes.
Start treating yourself like someone worth showing up
for—
because you are.

The moment you begin loving yourself
is the moment everything starts to shift.

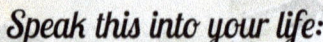

Speak this into your life:
From now on, I will show up for myself—I start by loving myself first.

If No One Told You Today...

If no one told you today...
Let me remind you:
You are gorgeous!
You are valuable.
You matter deeply.
You are whole.
You are more than enough.

Speak to yourself with kindness.
Look at yourself with love.
Hold yourself with the gentleness you've been longing
for.

You don't need outside approval
to believe in your beauty.

So, if no one told you today—
I hope you tell yourself.

Speak this into your life:

"I affirm my beauty, my strength, and my wholeness—out loud."

Finally Some Fresh Air

You're good, babe.
You're really good.
You should celebrate, because you're finally free now.
You're safe now.
You can be yourself now.
You can finally breathe.
You have the time and space to keep growing.
You have the energy to manifest every dream and
desire.

You wanted peace?
Embrace it now!
You wanted to feel cherished, loved, and appreciated?
Expect it now!

Look at you:
Happier.
Smiling more.
Radiating joy.
Glowing brighter.
So blessed now!
You're more satisfied.
More in love with life.
Your thoughts are clearer.
Your heart feels lighter.

Go after your goals.
Keep improving.
You are strong.
You are brave.

And most of all...
Be proud of yourself.
You've stepped into your power now,
and you're blooming in your own time.

Speak this into your life:

I choose softness, strength and self- celebration every day.

Smile

Smile, babygirl.
Laugh about it. Be happy about it.
Be grateful it happened.
Give thanks!
You've been given another chance—
A chance to learn,
To grow,
To truly get to know yourself.
An opportunity to expand your mind and soul,
To TRUST the Almighty again.

Smile, babygirl.
SMILE!
You may not understand why I'm asking you to smile
while you're still hurting inside.
But you will.
One day, you will.
I promise!

Smile, beautiful.
Sweet soul of mine.
Show me those beautiful dimples on your cheeks.
Let me see the brightness in your eyes.
They carry the same light that lives in your future.

Leave the worry behind.
Let go of the sadness.
They don't belong in this new chapter.

You were created with courage, with strength,
With wisdom and brilliance.

So yes, babygirl—

KEEP SMILING!
Be present.
And just smile.

Speak this into your life:
I smile, even through the healing, because I know that
joy is still mine.

After The Storm Comes Sunshine

I am at peace.
Not because it was easy,
But because I survived what tried to destroy me.
The chaos has calmed.
The noise has faded.
And in stillness, I found myself again.

No more shrinking.
No more doubting.
The storm taught me how to breathe in the middle of the
mess.
It taught me to surrender.
To listen.
To rest.

I faced the storm
and I won.
This is my after.
This is my sunshine.
This is my peace.

Speak this into your life:

The storm has passed. I am the sunshine now.

You Will Win In The End

"*This is where the story shifts.
Because a woman rooted in
love and faith always wins in the end.*"

She Wins With Grace

God doesn't miss a thing-

Not the lies you endured,
not the sacrifices you made,
not the kindness you gave when it wasn't returned.
He sees it all.
The love you gave,
The battles you never spoke of,
the tears no one saw,
And the prayers you whispered in silence.
He knows your heart,
your truth,
your intentions,
And how deeply you care.

So, keep loving purely.
keep choosing light.
keep choosing integrity.
Move with purpose.
Keep your spirit clean and your head high.

Because in the end,
The pure hearted always win.

And your reward will be greater than the pain you
endured.

Speak this into your life:
When I walk in faith, I walk in power, and I always win.

He Tried To Break Me- I Bloomed

Don't harbor hate for him-
Be grateful instead.
You needed that hurt to fuel your growth.
What he did didn't destroy you.
It was part of your journey,
It awakened you.
It pushed you to grow in ways comfort never could.
This is a lesson in strength, resilience and self-worth.
He didn't win.
He helped shape the woman who no longer settles,
no longer shrinks,
and no longer accepts less than she deserves.
That pain?
It was the beginning of your bloom.
And now look at you-
rooted in truth,
rising in power,
glowing with grace.

Trust me,
he only helped you discover your power.

Speak this into your life:

Blooming is my revenge and my reward.

Rejoice

It's your winning season.
Walk boldly into the blessings that are already yours.

Speak this into your life:
My breakthrough is here, and I am ready to embrace it.

Lesson Learned

The lesson hit hard
But you hit harder.
Look at you now.
you are not the same
You've grown.
You've earned your insight.
You've seen the truth.
Now you move different.
You don't doubt yourself anymore.
You walked through fire, and came out golden.

You are wiser in the most beautiful way!

Speak this into your life:

Because I've learned, I'll never settle again.

God Removed Him For You

God Had to clear the way,
Removing what didn't serve you,
so your real king could arrive.

The road had to be made clear,
so your heart could recognize what is truly meant for
you.
Sometimes, it takes losing what's not for you,
so that what's meant for you can find its way.

Trust that God is preparing your heart.
Clearing the path for the love that will honor you,
The love you truly deserve.

Speak this into your life:

*I honor my worth and trust that what's meant for me will come
when it's meant to.*

Surrender to Win

It's a new day.
It's a new life.

You're more aware of your worth now.
You see your value more clearly.

Accept this new life with faith
Embrace the new changes, and keep growing babygirl

I'm taking you to the top.
He can't even reach you anymore-

Trust me,

Your future is so bright!

So, whatever is falling apart right now,
Let it be!
Pick yourself up
and
Surrender to the divine plan.

Breath

and let go.

I love you.

Speak this into your life:

I surrender and walk into everything I once prayed for.

Clarity Crowned Her

I don't want chocolate and roses.
They won't relieve the pain.
Those fancy, and expensive jewels all beautifully
wrapped up
won't heal my bruises.
I no longer settle for temporary pleasure disguised as
love.
It won't heal my mind, body or soul.
Save that apology and the fake tears.
Today, I choose freedom.
I choose growth.
I choose happiness.
Today, I choose to see through the illusions
that made me forget who I am.

Speak this into your life:
I choose myself today, and every day moving forward.

She finally Broke Free

Today,
I won't have to wonder what I did so wrong
to deserve so much hate from someone
who claimed that I was the love of their life.
I won't have to question my worth or value
based on how the one that I loved so much treated me.
Today,
there's no need to walk around in fear for my safety.
I won't have to be cautious about what I say.
There will be no consequences.
Today,
No one will beat me.
nobody is cheating on me.
No one will call me crazy or delusional.
I won't be locked inside.
Today,
I don't have to hide my scars and bruises with make-up.
No one will tell me what to do.

Because today is the day that I am free.
Today
I can finally breathe a sigh of relief!

Speak this into your life:
Today I choose freedom, and I am reclaiming my life.

Your Revenge?
He can't touch you now

Heal.

because your healing is louder than your pain.

Let go.

not for him, but for your peace.

You don't owe the past anything.

Smile again.

because your joy?

It's the silence that echoes louder than any argument.

Don't respond.

Don't explain.

Your peace doesn't need proof.

Build.

a life so full,

his absence doesn't echo anymore.

Take that pain and mold it into purpose.

Let it move you,

not break you.

Draw the line.

Let your boundaries say,

"I will not bleed for someone who cuts for fun.

Forget his validation.

You were whole long before he came.

And you're still whole now.

Love yourself so loudly,

he hears it in his silence.

Because he was never worthy of it.

And when you rise,
step by step,
breath by breath—
Celebrate.
You made it!

Your revenge?
Is in your laughter.
In your softness returning.
In the safety you now feel.
In the love that surrounds you—
the real kind.
Because you're free now.
And there's nothing more powerful
than a woman
who never looks back.